Uncle Pete's
Pirate Adventure

Susannah Leigh

Illustrated by Brenda Haw

Edited by Louie Stowell
Cover design by Will Dawes

Contents

3 Make believe
4 The letter
6 Uncle Pete's boat
8 Pirates overboard!
10 Out to sea
12 Map reading
14 Shipmates
16 Look out!
18 The missing jewels
20 All hands on deck!
22 Jaggedy maze
24 Hide-and-seek pirates
26 A floating feast
28 Home again
30 A pirate story
31 Answers

Make believe

Mary and her friend Zac were playing pirates when they heard a knock. Mary rushed to open the door, but there was nobody there, just a letter on the doorstep...

This story is full of puzzles to solve.

If you get stuck there are answers on pages 31 and 32.

The letter

Dear  and , I need your help. Come to the and look for a like this. I will be on board. Don't forget to ask Mary's first! from

WELCOME LANDLUBBERS

4

"It's from Uncle Pete," said Mary.

"The pirate?" asked Zac. Mary had told him tales about Pete before. "What are we waiting for? Let's go!"

We're off to see Pete!

Bye Ma!

What does Uncle Pete's letter tell them to find?

5

Uncle Pete's boat

Mary and Zac raced down to the sea to find Uncle Pete's boat. But which one was it? There were so many!

Mary looked at the letter again.
"Uncle Pete's boat has a green steering
wheel and a blue flag," she said.
"There it is!" Zac cried.

Can you see Uncle Pete's boat?

Pirates overboard!

"Welcome aboard, me hearties," cried Uncle Pete.

Mary and Zac clambered into the little pirate boat and sat down. "We got your note," said Mary. "What's the problem, Uncle Pete?"

"I've lost my pirate crew," Uncle Pete replied. "Here's how it happened..."

There was a fierce storm at sea and my crew fell overboard. They swam to a nearby island, while I clung onto the boat's mast.

The storm died down, but by then I'd drifted miles away from the island. So I sailed home and mended my damaged boat.

"But you didn't *finish* mending it!" cried Mary, in alarm.

Can you see what Mary spotted?

Out to Sea

"Well spotted," said Uncle Pete, covering up the hole with pirate sticking tape. "Now, I have to rescue my crew. Will  you help me sail my boat to the island?" Zac and Mary nodded, eagerly.

"I'll take the wheel," said Pete. "Mary, you can read the map and Zac can keep lookout. There are lots of boats to dodge before we reach the open sea, but we can do it!"

Can you find a safe way out to sea?

11

Map reading

When they were safely on their way, Mary spread out the map. "Which island is your crew marooned on, Uncle Pete?" she asked.

"I can't remember its name, but I'm sure it had a volcano," said Pete.

Double Trouble Island

Rock Island

Spooky Isle

Barrel of Laughs Island

Monkey Island

Rumbling Tum Island

"And I know we passed some dolphins... and I had to sail around some jaggedy rocks," he added. "There were red jellyfish swimming around us, too."

Mary inspected the map. "There's only one island it could be."

Which island is it?

Uncle Pete's map of the Islands
(not to scale)

Firecracker Island

Flagpole Island

Pancake Island

Tall Trees Island

Prickly Pea Island

Shipmates

They set sail for Prickly Pea Island right away. As the wind blew them across the waves, Uncle Pete told Zac and Mary about his lost pirate crew.

Dave Doubloon is our navigator. He has a beard. **Betty Buccaneer** is my second in command. **Lester Lagoon** is our lookout man.

My pirate crew

"Your lookout man has an eyepatch!" said Zac. "But I suppose he only needs one eye to use his telescope."

How does Zac know what Lester Lagoon looks like?

15

Look out!

Zac scrambled up to the
crow's nest to do his lookout duty.
"Nothing to report, Cap'n," he called.

But when Zac looked again, the picture wasn't quite as calm. Someone was in trouble.

Who's in trouble? Can you spot all the differences between the two pictures?

The missing jewels

PEEP! Uncle Pete blew his special shark-scaring whistle and the sharks swam away.

But, just then, a big boat sailed up beside them. "This is the royal boat of Princess Scatterbrainia," called the captain. "Her jewels are missing. Can you help us find them?"

"We're pirates," called Zac. "So we're good at finding gold and jewels!"

"What has she lost?" called Mary.

"A sparkly gold necklace, a red bracelet and a jewel-studded crown," replied the captain, sounding worried.

"Don't panic," said Mary. "The princess's jewels are still on board. Look!"

Can you find the royal jewels?

All hands on deck!

The princess gave a regal wave as her ship sailed away. Suddenly, there was a shout – a steamboat was puffing up behind them.

"Swashbuckling sword fights!" cried Pete. "Bad Luck Bill's aboard that boat! He's the meanest pirate on the high seas!"

"And I think he's going to board us," cried Mary, in terror.

"Yikes!" yelped Zac.

Bad Luck Bill leaped onto their boat, brandishing his gleaming cutlass. Mary and Zac backed into a corner. They were in trouble now. But Zac had spotted something. "We're not the only ones in danger," he whispered.

What has Zac spotted?

Ha ha! Give me all your treasure, Uncle Pete. You're bound to have some.

Jaggedy maze

The octopus curled its
tentacle around the wicked
pirate's ankle and tugged. SPLASH!
Bad Luck Bill was in the water,
cursing and spitting.

"Bad luck, Bad Luck Bill!" Mary
chuckled. Then she looked at
the map again. "We're almost
at Prickly Pea island. Zac,
look out for the jaggedy
rocks!" she warned. "Pete,
you'll have to steer carefully."

*Can you see a path through the
jaggedy rocks to the island?*

Hide-and-seek pirates

Uncle Pete steered them safely through the maze of rocks until, finally, they came to Prickly Pea Island. They dropped their anchor and leaped ashore.

"It's quiet on this island," said Uncle Pete, with a frown. "Too quiet. Where's my crew?"

"Perhaps they're hiding?" said Mary. "Just in case we're enemy pirates."

They looked high and low.

"Aha!" Zac cried at last. "Come out, pirates, I can see you!"

Where are Dave Doubloon, Lester Lagoon and Betty Buccaneer?

A floating feast

The pirates came out and each gave Pete
a hearty pirate hug and said thanks to the
children. Then everyone clambered back
onto the boat and sailed away.

"Ahoy, Pete," called Betty Bucaneer, from
below decks. "Do you have any ship's
biscuits? There was nothing to eat
but slimy jellyfish on
that island!"

"I can do better than that, me hearties," replied Uncle Pete, with a twinkle in his eye. "There's wobbly green Jolly Roger dessert, swashbuckling sandwiches, captain's chocolate cake, and landlubbers lemonade and pirate pop to drink. But I'm not sure where I put it all."

"We'll find it!" said Zac.

Can you help find the pirate feast?

Limes

Lemonade

Home again

Soon, they reached the shore. Pete's pirate crew said goodbye. "We have pirate chores to do," said Betty. "Parrots to feed, flags to hoist, that sort of thing."

"But I'm sure we'll meet again soon," said Dave.

"Very soon," said Uncle Pete.

Back at Mary's house, her mother gave them cherry cake. As they were munching away, Zac's parents arrived at the door.

"It's time to go home," said his dad.

Zac yawned and nodded. "Life on the open seas is hard work!" he said. "Bye!"

Ahoy there matey... I mean, Son.

A pirate story

That night, Uncle Pete read Mary a swashbuckling pirate bedtime story.

"That was good," said Mary, sleepily. "But our pirate adventure was better."

"That's because it had *real* pirates in it," said Pete, with a sly little smile.

Answers

Pages 4-5
Mary and Zac have to find Uncle Pete's boat at the port.

Pages 6-7
Uncle Pete's boat is here.

Pages 8-9
Mary and Zac have spotted a hole in Uncle Pete's boat. Water is gushing through it!

Pages 10-11
The safe way to the open sea is shown in black.

Pages 12-13
Uncle Pete's pals are on Prickly Pea Island. It is the only island that matched Uncle Pete's description.

Pages 14-15
Zac has seen this picture of Uncle Pete's pirate crew.

Pages 16-17

The differences are circled in black. The windsurfer is in trouble.

Pages 18-19

The princess's jewels are circled in black.

Pages 20-21

Zac has spotted an octopus curling its tentacle around Bill's leg.

Pages 22-23

The way through the jaggedy rocks to the island is shown in black.

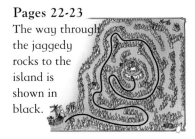

Pages 24-25

The six red jellyfish are circled in black.

Here is Dave Doubloon.   Here is Lester Lagoon.   Here is Betty Buccaneer.

Pages 26-27

The food and drink for the pirate feast are circled in black.

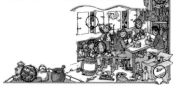

Pages 28-29

Did you spot something familiar about Zac's parents?

Page 30

Where have you seen Mary's dad before?

This edition first published in 2007 by Usborne Publishing Ltd., Usborne House, 83-85 Saffron Hill, London EC1N 8RT, England. www.usborne.com Copyright © 2007, 2002, 1995 Usborne Publishing Ltd. The name Usborne and the devices ⚓ 🎈 are Trade Marks of Usborne Publishing Ltd. All rights reserved.